LISA RAMOS *of* MTV's GUY CODE

...Pizza & Chill? 😉

HOW TO KINDA SORTA DATE

Dedication:

To my mom. Thanks for tolerating my shenanigans for the past two and a half decades. I love you!

*"Enjoy going through life
as yourself."*

- Lena Dunham, Girls

Table of Contents

Introduction

Dating for millennials is unlike any dating experience of the past. It can be fun, exciting, confusing, strange, disappointing, fulfilling, heart breaking— I could go on and on! Trying to understand dating in this day and age is like a goldfish trying to understand how a microwave functions. Yikes!

I've had my fair share of great, strange, and horrific experiences. Needless to say it has been a roller coaster ride! Luckily, I've been graceful enough to get through the odd times and fortunate enough to have had some amazing ones too. My hope for this book is that you'll learn about my experiences and know that you are not alone in this strange era where social media, celebrity culture, music, and society's ever-changing moral compass has made dating really weird!

Once, I went on a date with a guy who casually brought up that he had a girlfriend in the middle of our meal and great conversation. He was like, "Yeah, my girlfriend loves that movie, too." Then there was that one guy and his pet squirrels who was a great kisser, but ended up making headlines for a horrific crime. Thankfully, after our third date, I stopped replying to his texts about finally meeting his "kids" (aka the squirrels) and going over to Netflix and Chill. No Netflix and Chillin' for us, buddy!

While there have been some crazy experiences, I've had some really awesome ones, too! Great first dates, passion, exciting honeymoon stages, roses, spontaneous trips, awesome kissers, lots of laughs and love. I've had beautiful cliché walks on the beach, romantic picnics, adorable surprises (my ex bought me a bunny, two dogs, and a fish— he knew how much I loved animals!), meaningful conversations, and so many of those little moments that you don't realize are going to be the big and most memorable moments of your life.

Whether you are single, in a relationship, or serial dating, I believe you will find my honest tales and advice relatable, funny, and helpful. Here we go!

xoxo, Lisa

Everybody is Single at Some Point

"If you don't act like you've been hit by the plague when you're alone on a Friday night, and just see it as a chance to have fun by yourself, it's not a bad day."

—Taylor Swift

S ingle as a Pringle? Single and ready to mingle? Single and ready to complain about it on social media all day? The truth is, however you're handling being single, you are not alone. We've all been single at some point! It's the time to do whatever the heck you want. Do you want to go to live abroad in China? Do it. Do you want to fall off the face of the earth for a month? Go for it. Do you want to go to Vegas every weekend and act like you were raised in the jungle? You can! You're single. You only have to worry about yourself. And while being single is fun, sometimes it can get lonely. Cue the boyfriend-girlfriend pillow and the numerous orders from Domino's for a party of one! It's a double-edged sword.

When I was in college, I was three years into a relationship with my high school sweetheart. The relationship was wonderful until he decided he wanted to be single for the rest of his college experience. So, in a nutshell, he broke up with me and I was heartbroken. I listened to Daughtry's "Over You" on repeat. I cried. I called my aunt. I threw all his stuff in a trash bag only to keep it in the corner of my room because I wasn't ready to throw it out. While I was busy being melancholic and devastated, he was LOVING the single life... for about two weeks. Then he came back and tried to call the break up off, but it was too late. I was talking to someone new and going to visit him in Miami that same week. That guy ended up becoming my next boyfriend just a few weeks later. But that's beside the point. The moral of the story is that it's better to be single than in an unhappy relationship. Being in a relationship when you want to be single isn't right. Being in a relationship with someone who wishes to be single isn't right. That went for both of us.

10 Best Things about Being Single

1 You can come and go as you please! You don't have to check in with anyone or update anyone on your whereabouts.

2 You can see as many people as you want! You can check out new restaurants, movies, museums, and events every week with a new person.

3 You have more time to hang out with your friends. You can plan trips, go to brunch, and make spontaneous plans whenever you'd like. Oh, and your friends can't complain about never seeing you because of your significant other!

4 You get the whole bed to yourself. No sharing with a blanket hog or snoring beast!

5 You always have something funny to share with your friends about the weird or crazy dates you've been on. My friends live vicariously through me when I'm single.

You can go to bed not worrying about your significant other being out or drinking with their friends. You only have yourself to worry about.

 You can stay out as late as you want or never go home at all because there is no one waiting up for a call or text saying you're home safely.

 Your room can be as messy as you want. No one will be around to complain about it!

 You can post whatever you want on social media without worrying what your significant other and their family will think about it!

 You don't have anyone being nosey about your finances or getting on your case about pointless, frivolous spending. If you go broke, it's your problem!

Let me put some of my experiences to the test and help you guys out. Throughout each chapter of this book, you'll find questions that I've been receiving from fans of **Guy Code** since *forever*. The idea is that some of my insights might help you guys out in your own dating lives. I'll share what I've "learned" and maybe you'll learn from my mistakes... or maybe you'll just laugh at the incredibly clumsy way I would handle certain dating scenarios. 😊

**Q: I've been single for a while…
too long really. My friends
keep pushing me to try online
dating, but it seems like it's
only for old people (and a little
embarrassing). Should I try it?**

A: What do you have to lose? People of
all ages are on dating apps. People say it's
like going to a bar without having to leave
your house or get ready. I actually know
two couples who met on dating apps.
They've been together for over a year! I
say try it. If you hate it, delete it.

**Q: How do you stay confident
when approaching a guy you like?
Is it okay to make the first move?**

A: I'm really shy so I've never approached
a guy. I like being sure a guy is interested
because *he approached me*. But I say just
go for it! Approach him as if you guys are
friends with a smile on your face. Keep in
mind that rejection is possible. He may be
taken, gay, or simply not interested.

Q: How many times is it okay to text someone without a response before giving up?

A: The magic number is 3. Sometimes people get busy. They forget to reply. They weren't in the mood to speak that day. Their phone malfunctions. They were thinking about getting back with their ex. They were mad at you. Whatever. It's normal not to get a reply every so often. However, if you text someone on three occasions* and do not get a response, it is time to fold! I went on two dates with a man who texted me 87 times over the course of a year with no response. I was going to block him but keeping count was kind of fun.

*By three occasions, I mean three different days. Texting someone three times in the same moment still counts as one occasion. For example: **Text 1**: Hey Lisa! **Text 2**: I just passed by your favorite restaurant and thought of you. **Text 3**: So how are you? Even though that's three texts, it counts as one occasion.

Q: Is the pick-up line "I lost my number, can I have yours?" okay to use on a girl or is it corny?

A: Corny! You shouldn't break the ice by asking for a phone number immediately. You ask for her number at the end of the conversation. It's always best to ask for a phone number when one of you is about to leave. This way, if she says "no", you're not awkwardly hanging around each other after the rejection.

Q: How do you help your newly single best friend get over their ex?

A: Make plans! Go out, have fun, and keep your best friend busy. An idle mind will delay the process.

Q: Is it okay to hang out with someone new two days in a row or should you space it out?

A: It depends. If you're visiting each other from out of town, hanging out a few days in a row is totally okay because you won't see each other again for a while. However, if you live in the same state, I think it's better to space things out. You don't want to wear out your welcome in someone's personal space and free time.

Q: How much of an age difference do you think is okay when dating?

A: I think 10 years older is the cut off in age difference if you're in your 20's. If you're younger than 20, I think 3 years older is the cut off. The gap gets bigger the older you get. Funny how that works.

Q: Is it okay to date someone who looks amazing but you don't have any chemistry with... you know, just for fun?

A: No, it's wrong to date selfishly. When you date someone solely for their looks or any other shallow aspect, you're indifferent to the collateral damage you'll do to their feelings. It's not okay to manipulate someone's thoughts or emotions for your own instant gratification.

Q: Do you believe in the 3 day rule/taking a long time to text back rule?

A: This rule is stupid. 😑 That's all I have to say about it.

Q: Is it okay to meet people online?

A: In this day in age, it is very normal to meet people online via apps and social media. My advice is to use wisdom if you want to go this route. Meet in a public, well-lit place. Do **NOT** go to someone's home or have someone come to yours, even if it is just to pick you up. If my friends ever want to meet someone from the internet, I have them send me the name, phone number, and photo of the person. I suggest you do the same. Horrific things can happen if you're not careful. Also, if you're under 18, **DO NOT EVER** meet anyone offline, period!

Q: So there is this guy I really like and we have been "talking" for a few months, but I find myself texting him first all the time and we will even go days without texting. This really pisses me off! What should I do?

A: Nothing. You should do nothing. If the effort isn't being reciprocated, you need to back away. If he doesn't pick up the slack then he simply isn't as interested as you are. End it and move on.

Q: Is serial dating okay?

A: Serial dating is definitely okay! The only rule is that you be honest with the people you are dating. They don't need to know *all* the details, but they should know that you aren't seeing them exclusively. Being honest makes things much easier. It would be awkward to have someone you're seeing bump into you in public while you're on another date if they don't know you're seeing other people. It's best to avoid that kind of drama and be upfront about what's going on.

Q: What are some ways to know if someone is starting to like you?

A: Someone's effort to speak to you and see you is a reflection of their interest in you. If they always want to talk to you and see you, they probably like you. Another telltale sign is that they remember small details about you that other people don't notice.

Q: How do I make the first move to kiss my friend? I like her, and I think she likes me. I think if I kiss her and she goes for it, I'll know for sure. How do I go about it?

A: Whoa, don't just kiss her out of nowhere! Start slow. Watch a movie at home together. See if she's okay with sharing a blanket and doing some cuddling. If she doesn't pull away or say "Ew! Omg, wtf are you doing, nasty?!" then you can try kissing her. If she slaps you or throws up, just laugh it off and keep being friends.☺

Q: This girl I have a huge crush on told me that she's not interested. What should I do?

A: Nada! Move on to someone who is interested in you. You can't *make* someone like you, and any attempts to do so will be absolutely futile. You should give your time to people who feel the same way about you.

Q: I really like my friend's ex-girlfriend. He's not my best friend, but we are all in the same circle. Should I go for it? Should I ask him for permission? Help!

A: What?! No way! There are certain boundaries you should not cross. Friends' exes and former flings are *absolutely off limits*. There are plenty of fish in the sea. Leave that fish alone, STAT! That is completely against the rules in my circle of friends. Once one of my friends even *thinks* someone is attractive, they are off limits to everyone else in the group. Things work better that way.

Chapter 1 Playlist

SHE DON'T WANNA MAN - ASHER ROTH FT. KERI HILSON

NO SCRUBS - TLC

IT'S MY LIFE - BON JOVI

I'M SINGLE - LIL WAYNE

YOUNG WILD & FREE - SNOOP DOGG FT. WIZ KHALIFA

U + UR HAND - PINK

RIDIN SOLO - JASON DERULO

YOU DON'T HAVE TO CALL - USHER

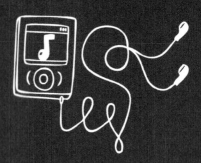

Dating Yourself First

"*Some people said, 'Oh. You don't want to be alone.' And I said, "I'm not alone! I'm with myself. And myself is fabulous."*"

—Eva Longoria

You've got to *love yourself first* before you can invest in any kind of relationship. I know it sounds like a basic, girly Instagram quote (with a white background and black lettering with a caption reading "THIS.") but it could not be truer. I mean, why would anyone feel obligated to treat you better than you treat yourself? *You* set the standard for how you are to be treated by how you care for and treat yourself.

If you feel confident, you are less likely to accept poor treatment from others. This is why self-care is a must. Work out. Groom yourself. Read books. Get enough sleep. Pray. Be kind to yourself. Only say nice things about yourself. Surround yourself with positive people. Encourage yourself daily with a little pep talk in the mirror. You are valuable, smart, gifted, equipped, and anyone would be lucky to have you as a friend or significant other! Anyone who makes you feel otherwise is not worth a millisecond of your time.

There have been plenty of times when I've felt sad, discouraged, and not good enough. Most of the time, after a quick evaluation of my thoughts and feelings, I realized that the people I was spending most of my time with sucked. Don't be afraid to cut people off who make you feel like you are hard to love, hang out with, or be around. This goes for friends, significant others, co-workers, etc. *It ain't nun to cut that...* I won't finish the lyric but if you know the song, you catch my drift. 😐

My point is you're awesome. You should only give your time to people who believe that, too.

10 Ways to Love on Yourself

Speak to yourself kindly. Say 3 positive things about yourself out loud. You have more good qualities than you think!

Get into a new television show. It feels good to be entertained by a fictional world for 30 minutes a day, or 8 hours a day if you're binge watching!

Take care of your body. Get some exercise and do your best to eat healthy.

Give yourself some alone time. Read a book at the park, go on a hike, and take photos of beautiful scenery. It's important to learn to enjoy your own company.

Clean your home/room. You'll feel so much better if your personal space is clean and in order.

Read books! The best thing you can do is feed and exercise your brain by filling it with knowledge.

 Fill your room with things that are pleasing to your senses, like a great scented candle, a lamp with cool lighting, a cozy bed set, a calming playlist, etc.

 Eliminate people and things that cause you to feel badly about yourself. Anyone or anything that isn't having a positive impact on your life needs to go!

 Limit your time on social media. It causes insecurity and misplaced envy. It's normal to compare yourself to others on social media, but we forget that we are seeing highlights of their lives. We should not be jealous of what we don't actually know!

 Make a weekly "To Do" list. You'll feel great using your time to be productive and accomplishing your short and long term goals.

Q: Do you ever go on dates by yourself, like to the movies or to dinner?

A: I sure do! I travel alone for work a lot so I go to restaurants by myself quite often. I enjoy dining alone now. I have over 500 bookmarks on Yelp so I always have a new place to try. I've never been to the movies alone, though.

Q: How do I know if I am ready to start dating after a long relationship?

A: In my opinion, you are ready to start dating when you are no longer dwelling on your past. It is good to take time to really get over your past relationship before getting into a new one. Otherwise, it's just a pointless rebound.

Q: My ex keeps texting me and I kinda want to answer him, but we broke up because we just didn't fit well. What should I do?

A: I heard someone once say "When the past starts calling, let it go to voicemail!"

If you're sure there's no chance of reconciliation, just ignore the texts and calls. If you weren't a good match then, you won't be a good match now.

You're still the same people with the same personalities, beliefs, friends, families, and lives. No need to try to make those puzzle pieces fit together again if you've already tried. I say ignore him and find someone better suited for you.

"*Before you diagnose yourself with depression or low self-esteem, first make sure that you are not, in fact, surrounded by assholes.*"

— William Gibson

Q: Do you think it is okay for me and my girlfriends to take a girl's trip? My boyfriend seems to be bothered by it, but I really want to go.

A: There's nothing wrong with a girl's trip. Let him know you're okay with keeping in touch with him during the trip. Both parties in every relationship should have room to hang out with friends and family without trivial restrictions. This means a boy's trip would be okay for him too. Fair is fair.

Q: Am I selfish for breaking up with my ex because we're going to different colleges?

A: Not at all! If you feel that was the right decision, then it was. It's better to be single than to reluctantly stay in a relationship. Plus, your college years are your first years of real freedom. Enjoy them without restrictions! 😊

Q: I'm in a bad relationship with my girl. We fight and makeup and fight and makeup all the time. When we're good, we're good, but we seem to fight so much. Should we end it? I do think she's the one... What do I do?!

A: If you think she's *the one*, then the relationship is worth fighting for. Relationships go through rough seasons from time to time. Have a talk and try to figure out what the root of all the arguing is. Once you figure that out, you have a better chance at solving the real problem and attaining some peace.

Chapter 2 Playlist

VIDEO GIRL - INDIA ARIE

GREATEST LOVE OF ALL - WHITNEY HOUSTON

JUST THE WAY YOU ARE - BRUNO MARS

ONE IN A MILLION - NEYO

FEELING GOOD - NINA SIMONE

The Perfect First Date

"A man in Detroit was sentenced to two years in prison for stealing a woman's car after skipping out on the check on their first date. I don't know what's sadder, the fact that he did that, or the fact that she's still counting it as a date."

– Seth Meyers

First dates are kind of like job interviews. You show up, look your best, and only say half of what you're actually thinking. If you're lucky, your date does the same. Like Forrest Gump once said: "First dates are like a box of chocolates. You never know what you're going to get!" He said that, right? Well, he said something like that and it's true! First dates are nerve-wracking for a lot of people because you really have no clue how it's going to go. You have to just get there, put your seatbelt on, and prepare for what could be a bumpy ride.

I once went on a first date with a guy I met through a friend who wanted to make out within the first FIVE MINUTES of the date. I mean its fine to want to make out, but you can't expect your date to be down for that right away! I was like, "Um, let's go get some food first. I'm starving." When we got to the restaurant, I made sure I ordered a steak sandwich with EXTRA onions. Oh, and by the way, he still *tried* to kiss me after my onion feast and said, "Mmmm, I love onions." Gross.

On another first date, it was total *like-at-first-sight*. He was tall, dark, and handsome. He smelled amazing, and was waiting for me outside his car with a blue rose and a gigantic Reese's peanut butter cup (he knew from our previous text conversations that those were my favorite). We went to a local coffee shop and talked and laughed for hours, followed by a trip to In-N-Out's drive through. It was by no means a fancy date, but honey, when he dropped me off at home I was so deep in like with him that I was in a loopy mood for *hours*. I was high off infatuation. Ask my best friend! She was there to witness the hysteria. It didn't go much further than that because we weren't very compatible, but it was definitely a great first date!

First Date Etiquette:
5 Do's & 5 Don'ts

 Do be on time! If you're running late, call your date and let them know.

 Do be open to different date ideas. A picnic in the park, Dave & Busters, Indoor Sky Diving, an interactive Broadway show, etc.

 Do make a reservation. It would be awkward to have to stand around waiting to be seated for 40 minutes.

 Do be nice and pleasant. No need to discuss horrific current events or a sad story about your past. The point of a first date is to have fun together!

 Do dress to impress! You don't have to show up in formal wear, but it is nice to be on a date with someone who put some thought into their appearance.

Don't go to a second location if you're not enjoying the date. It's better if you politely say that you're ready to go home.

 Don't admit to stalking your date on social media. If you know everything there is to know about your date already, what is there to talk about?

 Don't be on your phone the whole time. Your texts, unimportant calls, and social media apps can be put on hold for the few hours that you're with your date.

 Don't forget gum and mints! You don't know if there will be any closeness or kissing happening.

 Don't be pushy. If you suggested a second location, initiated a kiss, or tried to hold their hand and they didn't respond positively, just let it be. They will open up at their own pace, if/when they feel comfortable.

Q: What should I do on a first date? I have a first date soon and I want it to be fun.

A: I love fun first dates! You can't go wrong with a fun activity and food, in whatever order. You can go play pool, an arcade, sporting event, or theme park.

Q: What kind of restaurant should I take this girl I like for our first date?

A: Ask her what her favorite kind of food is and go off that. You should pick the place and make the reservation, but it's absolutely fine to ask for her food preference. If she hits you with the typical "I don't care. You pick!" line, then pick a place that's within your budget that has burgers, salads, chicken, and pasta on the menu. Everyone loves at least one of those things!

Q: How do you get out of a date that you can tell is going nowhere 15 minutes into it?

A: Easy! You fake a phone conversation. ☺ Text any one of your close friends and say, "Call me ASAP." When they call you, totally fake a conversation no matter what your friend is saying on the other line.

For example: Phone rings. You pick up. "Hey! Oh my God— what?! When? That's crazy. Are you okay? Should I come now? Oh my goodness! Okay just stay put. I'll head over. No, it's fine. I'm on my way. Yes. Okay. Yes. Okay. Okay. Bye." If your friend is smart, they'll catch on. If not, just explain later!

Q: Is it okay to text my girls during a date or should I be discrete and run to the bathroom to update them?

A: You shouldn't text during your date. Put your phone away and really be present so you can see if you really click with your date. Send a quick update when your date goes to the bathroom.

If you run to the bathroom to update them more than once, your date might think you have a UTI or a stomachache.😣

Q: I just got out of a long (3 year) relationship. I'm going on a first date with this guy I met, but I'm rusty. Any tips?

A: Aw, good! It should be fun to start dating again. **My tips are:**

- Look great so you feel great.
- Don't talk about your ex.
- Be yourself!

Q: What are better date options than just dinner and a movie? I really want to impress the girl I'm taking out.

A: Dates don't have to be fancy to be great. They just have to be fun. You can go mini-golfing, bowling, an arcade, a pottery class, a sporting event, a Broadway show, etc. However, there should always be food involved. I'm like an infant— I'm happy as long as I'm fed and kept warm.

Q: How can I cancel a date last minute without seeming bitchy? I said yes out of pity. I don't find him attractive.

A: That's what happens when you're not honest. You find yourself in awkward situations. Last minute cancellations require a phone call. Let him know you can no longer make it. And for future reference, you're never obligated to say "yes" to anything you're not comfortable with. "No, thank you" is a perfectly good answer. This goes for men and women.

Q: Ordering dessert on the first date. Yes or no?

A: Yes, yes, and yes! I'll take whatever chocolate dessert is on the menu, please!

Q: What are some red flags on first dates? What is the biggest red flag you've ever seen?

A: **Some red flags on first dates include:**

- Talking about their ex
- Asking inappropriate questions that make you uncomfortable
- Rude behavior toward people around you
- Heavy drinking
- Arriving more than 20 minutes late
- Oversharing personal information*
- Constantly checking their phone

*I was having a great first date with this really handsome, charming guy. The conversation and wine was flowing. Then suddenly, halfway through my chicken pad thai, he started spilling all this shocking information. I learned that he had been arrested 6 times, owned 4 guns, and got the huge scar on his hand from a nearly lethal fight in a hotel room after a night out at a strip club. W.T.F. right!? Red flags were all over the place, but all I did was smile and say, "Wow!" There was nothing he could say to redeem himself. I had already decided that I would not be going on another date with this sexy psycho and his stupid beautiful green eyes and tattoos.

Q: When is a good time to call a girl after a first date?

A: Immediately is fine, actually. You can call her to make sure she got home safely and say you had a nice time. If you dropped her off, you can call her the next day. If you wait too long, it can be off-putting. Definitely send that "good night" text, though. We love that. 😵

Q: Does a pizza place on a first date come off as cheap?

A: It depends what the style of the date is. If you're going to a street fair or carnival, pizza is fine. Just be clear about where you're going. Don't let your date get all dressed up to go to a local pizza parlor.

Q: What's the worst date you've ever been on?

A: Oh gosh, this is a looong one...

This guy took me to get sushi and walk on the Santa Monica Pier. He was handsome and smart. I thought it was going to go really well.

On the way there, he was driving like a maniac. He was determined to make it to our reservation on time, but I was terrified. Then at dinner, I noticed he was taking sneaky photos of me! Not only that, he kept asking to take a selfie with me. I politely declined and he got upset.

He then made a joke about how *he* was the one paying for dinner so *he* should choose what to share for dessert. I immediately took out my card and said, "Ha, no worries. I got this." He apologized immediately and said he was "just" joking. He also kept making jokes about how we were going to kiss. I would've rather made out with a rattlesnake.

As we were walking to his car after dinner, he insisted that I looked cold (I was freezing, actually) and wanted to have his arms around me. *Yuck, no! I would rather freeze to death, thanks.*

It wasn't long before I realized we'd been walking for a while and we hadn't reached his car yet. He claimed that he didn't remember where we parked. I told him it was no problem and that I'd call an Uber. He instantly said, "No! I lied. I just wanted more time with you so I didn't want to get to the car yet." I'd rather not share what I told him after that. Let's just say he was as quiet as a mouse on the way to my place.

Needless to say, I blocked him as soon as I got home. It was the worst date ever.

Q: Does it matter what you order on a first date?

A: I wouldn't order the most expensive bottle of wine and dish, but you also don't have to get a house salad and water. If your date picked the place, they can afford it.

Q: Is the first date too soon to bring up past relationships?

A: Yes! First dates are meant to be light, breezy, and fun. Don't make it weird and turn it into a therapy session.* Just have fun and enjoy each other's company!

*I went on a first date where my date disclosed all this personal information about his exes, his family, his childhood, etc. I was so taken back, I didn't know what to say. The majority of the date was me saying, "Oh, my God." and "Wow!" and "I'm sorry to hear that." By the time I got home, I needed a couple glasses of wine and therapy myself! We had one more date (I shouldn't have bothered, but he was so ridiculously good looking I wanted to give him another shot 😶) where he told me the craziest story about 1 of the 5 times he got arrested. That was IT for me! I never saw him again. He should've waited 'til I was in love with him to reveal that he was nuts! No but really, take your time discussing your personal life. Not everyone deserves to get to know you so well.

Chapter 3 Playlist

LOVE IN THIS CLUB - USHER

GET LUCKY - DAFT PUNK

I GOTTA FEELING - BLACK EYED PEAS

DANCING IN THE MOONLIGHT - VAN MORRISON

YOU'RE THE ONE THAT I WANT - GREASE SOUNDTRACK

THE WAY YOU MAKE ME FEEL - MICHAEL JACKSON

BOW CHICKA WOW WOW - MIKE POSNER FT. LIL WAYNE

WONDERFUL TONIGHT - ERIC CLAPTON

Heart Break

"*Pour yourself a drink, put on some lipstick, and pull yourself together.*"

— *Elizabeth Taylor*

Breaking up effing sucks. Whether you are the one breaking someone's heart, or the one getting broken up with, it's not an easy thing to do. If you're the one ending the relationship, you can feel guilty, sad, nervous, and confused about whether you're making the right decision. When you're on the receiving end of the bad news, it can be shocking, devastating, infuriating, and also confusing. Sometimes, the break up is mutual and both parties go on their separate ways, with some pain, but for the most part ready to start a new chapter in their lives. One thing I can guarantee is that no matter who you are in the situation, you will be absolutely fine!

After my first break up with my high school/college sweetheart, I was devastated. I did not think I would find anyone like him. I was so sad and could not believe he was letting me go, just like that *(snaps fingers)*. He wanted to run wild like a gorilla in the jungle and do all the fun things young, handsome, student athletes do. I cried for two days straight before deciding I was going to get over it whether I liked it or not! I started making plans with my friends, went on a girl's trip, joined a gym, and made sure I was always busy and having fun. *Staying busy after a break up is key!* It was but one week before I was over it and into someone else.

But that's just one story. Break ups are as messy as they are unique. A different broken heart started with a bad fight. We were in a heated argument and he blurted out, "It's over!" Taking my past experiences into account, I left *our* apartment a few hours later to go shopping and never went back. Some people, when broken up with, try to hold onto the relationship until their knuckles turn white but I could not get away from this person fast enough. I ran like I stole something. I was so happy to have been released from the relationship. It was not where I wanted to be any longer and I am sure I would've broken it off sooner or later if he hadn't. Granted, he backtracked on his impulsive decision almost immediately and would *not* let me live in peace for a *long* time, but that's a whole different (and scary) story.

My point is, whether you're glad or devastated about the relationship ending, everything will be fine! You will move onto better, more suitable relationships. Think about it. If couples who have been married for 15+ years with kids, a home, two dogs, a picket fence, a timeshare in Mexico, a goldfish, and mutual friends can separate, move on, and be happy, you can too. Your best days are still ahead of you.

"You don't get to choose if you get hurt in this world... but you do have some say in who hurts you. I like my choices."

– John Green

10 Tips for
Mending a Broken Heart

 Indulge in a day of gluttony. I usually order a pizza pie just for me (stuffed crust from Pizza Hut if I'm really sad). Also an entire Entenmann's banana crunch cake does the soul good after a heartbreak.

 Listen to some sad songs and cry, and then some good angry music that makes you say "F*ck it!" about your ex.
Anger is sadness' bodyguard.

 Make plans for your week. Write down a plan for each day even if it's to binge watch your favorite show and drink some wine. A full schedule will make you feel better.

 Have a primping day!

Girls: get a manicure and pedicure, get your hair done, get a spray tan, etc.

Guys: Get your hair cut, hit the gym, buy a new outfit, etc.

 Stay off social media! Delete all your social apps. I recommend staying off for 5 days or more.

Go out with your friends. A good night out will remind you that it's fun to be single!

 Make a list of all the things that made you sad about the relationship. List all the things that were said and done that made you feel awful. After reading it, you'll be glad it's over.

 Throw away all the items in your home that have anything to do with your ex. If you're a really nice person, put them in a box for your ex to retrieve them. Personally, I prefer the first option.

 Do not, I repeat, DO NOT speak to your ex at all! Ignore all calls and texts. I understand this is impossible in some situations but limit the dialogue to an absolute minimum.

 Keep in mind that everything happens for a reason. If it didn't work out with this person, it is because someone better is on their way.

Q: My boyfriend broke up with me today. I'm in pieces. What should I do?

A: Cry it out until you feel better. I say 1-2 days of crying and moping is okay. After you get a good cry out of your system, it is time to start moving forward. When one door closes, another door opens. Don't block the entrance by dwelling over someone who does not want to be with you.

Q: I broke up with my ex because he was just not a good fit. But it hurt really badly and it was a messy breakup. Now I miss him! What do I do?

A: Nothing. You know he's not right for you. If you just resist the urge to contact him, it will eventually go away. Keep busy! Go on other dates, join a salsa class, hang out with your girlfriends, adopt a cat, join the Peace Corps, learn another language, become an astronaut, move to China, etc. Stay busy!

Q: My boyfriend just broke up with me in the meanest way possible. I'm in so much pain. Would it be terrible if I texted the nudes he sent me to his parents or friends?

A: That wouldn't do anything but cause more drama. Don't add any more negative thoughts or actions to the situation. In time, karma will reciprocate what he did better than you ever could. Trust me! No one can run from the consequences of their actions. Taking the high road may seem sucky, but I know from experience that it's always the best way to go.

Q: My boyfriend left me and I got fired from my job today, WTF?! How should I unwind from this shitty day?

A: Take a deep breath. This unfortunate chain of events is temporary. Nothing lasts forever, even the bad times. It'll be okay!

Q: What's the best way to break up with someone?

A: Just be brutally honest.* Honesty is truly the best policy. They may be upset but in hindsight they will appreciate it. And have the decency to do it face-to-face. Any other form of communication is lame and inappropriate for a break up.

*When I say "brutally" honest, I mean don't sugarcoat what you're feeling. I don't mean be brutally honest for the sake of being brutal. You can say, "I'm not as attracted to you as I once was." Don't say, "I think you're gross 😧, I hate the way you chew your food, your new haircut is stupid, you wear ugly sneakers and your cologne gives me a headache." You can be honest about the bottom line without giving too many details.

Q: Is dating someone new a good way to get over a broken heart?

A: There is nothing wrong with hanging out with someone new and having fun after a break up. However, make sure you take things slow and are careful not to jump into another relationship prematurely.

I know so many people who jump from relationship to relationship and are never really happy because they didn't get over the previous one. Take your time. You'll never regret taking things slow.

Q: Are guys immune to having their heart broken? I dated this guy for two years. We went through what I thought was a very painful breakup. He kept telling me I broke his heart. And now, three weeks later, he's dating a new girl and posting pictures of how happy they are together!? WTF!

A: Absolutely not. Men are just better at hiding their emotions. It sounds like this guy is trying to make you jealous. Oh, well! Onward you go. If you know you made the right decision, there is no reason to look back.

PS: Stop checking his social media! Stalking an ex won't do you any good, ever.

Q: How do you get over a broken heart?

A: It takes time! Grieving for a week or so is completely normal. After that period where you do nothing but sulk or cry, it's time to keep busy and get on with your life! Get up, get dressed, and go out with your friends, meet new people, plan fun weekly activities etc. Eventually you will have built a whole new amazing life without your ex! Everything will fall into place with time.

Q: What's the worst break-up you've ever gone through?

A: I'd say the one I mentioned earlier was the worst one. We lived together, shared dogs, our families got involved, he didn't accept that it was over and would *not* leave me alone for an entire year. His behavior became scary and unpredictable. I did everything I could to stay away from him! ☠

"If you want to fix a broken heart, friends make the best glue."

– Hannah Cheatam

Q: I cheated on my ex but they never found out. We broke up for a different reason. Should I tell them or should I leave it alone now that we're both over the heartache?

A: Yikes! 😨 Why would you fess up now? Don't add insult to injury. Keep that information to yourself.

Q: My girlfriend is moving away. Should we just end it? I don't think long distance relationships ever end with anything but heartbreak.

A: I know plenty of couples who have had successful long distance relationships. It takes a lot of effort, but it is possible. Actually, I had a lot of fun when I was in a long distance relationship. The visits were exciting. Absence really does make the heart grow fonder!

Q: My current GFs birthday is next week, but I want to break up. Should I wait until her birthday to not ruin it or do I do it beforehand to avoid her birthday all together?

A: That's a tough one. Truthfully, I would wait until after her birthday. When you do let her know you want to break up, do it face-to-face. Be gentle and respectful, but honest.

Chapter 4 Playlist

OVER YOU - DAUGHTRY

FUCK YOU - CEELO GREEN

COMFORTABLE - LIL WAYNE

BREAK UP - MARIO

I CAN SEE CLEARLY NOW - JOHNNY NASH

NOTHING BETTER - POSTAL SERVICE

SOMEONE SAVED MY LIFE TONIGHT - ELTON JOHN

DON'T WANNA BE YOUR GIRL - WET

SO SICK - NEYO

JUMP - RIHANNA

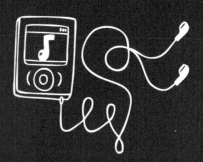

Love, Sex, Friends with Benefits & Respect

"Where am I going to meet an architect who lives in Brooklyn besides Tinder at this point? It's the modern-day singles bar."

—Andy Cohen

There is so much grey area when it comes to dating nowadays! Within these 50 Shades of Dating, there's online dating, friends with benefits, serial dating, gay dating, bi dating, exclusive dating, it goes on and on. There are so many kinds of dating preferences that websites like FarmersOnly.com and ChristianMingle.com even exist! Things can get pretty specific when it comes to peoples' preferences. Whatever your style, it's all good! To each their own. So, do whatever excites and works for you.

The one thing that should remain constant across all forms of dating, whether it's the old school way or some realm within this new dating era, is respect. You should always be sure to receive and give respect to those you are spending your time with. A lack of respect leads to dysfunction in your relationships, which will lead to disappointing feelings and situations. What's the point of dating if you're not enjoying one another's company? There is none. So make sure you expect respect and give it in return! We are all worthy of it.

Texting & Sexting: 5 Do's & 5 Don'ts

 Do send cute and fun photos that go with your text message! *For example:* Send a photo of the brownie sundae you're eating if s/he asked what you're up to.

 Do send sweet good morning and good night texts.

 Do show your personality. Make jokes. Boring text conversations end quickly and lead nowhere.

 Do use emoji's! They make the texts more fun and flirtatious.

 Do be direct. If you want to invite someone somewhere or want to discuss something, say it. Beating around the bush gets weird via text and things can get confusing quickly.

 **Don't** send unsolicited sexy photos. You don't know who the person is with at the moment and you don't know if they're ready to receive those from you.

 Don't begin or end every text with LOL, hahaha! or Lmao. The conversation isn't funny the whole entire time.

 Don't confuse "their", "they're" and "there". Major turn off!

 Don't forget to ask questions to keep the conversation going. If you never ask about the other person, they are likely to stop replying.

 Don't follow the "3 Day Rule". It's such an old trick, everyone knows exactly what's happening. A follow-up text right after a date is just fine.

Q: I've got this guy friend who I hook-up with occasionally. It's fun and spontaneous. But I really don't want him to fall for me and I don't want to fall for him. How can we avoid it?

A: Stop hooking up. Eventually, one of you will get more romantically involved than the other. Someone is going to get hurt. 😢

Q: How do I get my FWB to date me exclusively?

A: Talk to them about it. There's a chance you both may want more than just a FWB relationship. The only way to find out is to ask them how they feel. If they want to move forward, good. If not, end the "relationship" and move on. These interactions don't end well when both parties aren't on the same page.

Q: I've been on a few dates with this guy, but outside of a kiss, there's been no moves. How do I tell him that I want to get a little frisky?

A: First of all, this is a good thing. It means he respects you and is willing to go at your pace. Since you're ready to do more, all you have to do is let him know. I am sure he's waiting patiently for the green light.

Q: The girl I'm dating doesn't want me to meet her parents yet. I find it a little odd. Should I respect her wishes, or should I reach out to them?

A: You should respect her wishes. Reaching out would be creepy and disrespectful. What would you even say? You will meet them at the right time, and she will let you know when that is.

Q: How do I tell this girl that I want to be friends with benefits without making it feel like I'm just using her? We're good friends, so I don't want to ruin our friendship.

A: Just tell her the truth. Be very upfront and clear about your intentions. Honesty is the best policy!

Q: I want to end the "arrangement" I have with this guy because I just found out he has the same FWB arrangement with another girl. I know you're not supposed to get emotional in these situations but I did. What do I do?

A: I say just end it immediately. You're setting yourself up to get your feelings hurt. If this is how you feel now, imagine how you'll feel if you let it go on!

Q: How many dates should you go on before you kiss a guy?

A: When it comes to *kissing*, just go with the flow. I've kissed on the first date and I've been on numerous dates with the same guy and never kissed him. If it feels right and you feel comfortable and safe, go for it. Don't force it. Don't make it weird. Don't put yourself in a compromising position that causes you to feel uncomfortable or unsafe.

Q: I met my current boyfriend on Tinder. It's embarrassing to tell my friends and family how we met, but I'm positive we are going to slip up. Should we just fess up?

A: You don't have to be so specific! You can just say you met online. That can mean Facebook, Instagram, Twitter, etc. After you've been dating for a while, people will stop asking how you met. If all else fails, just change the subject by having a cough attack or pretending you forgot something important in your car.

Q: When is it okay to introduce a new partner to your friends and family? I don't want to do it too soon because I don't want them to feel rushed. If I take too long, does it look like I'm hiding something?

A: In my opinion, 3 months into exclusively dating is a good time to introduce someone to your friends and family.

Q: Sex with my girlfriend is amazing. But outside the bedroom, we are on different paths (career goals, views on politics, religion, everything). Should I end it? Do you think we could be FWB?

A: You don't have to end a relationship just because you don't share the same exact views and goals. If you truly love her, you can still make it work. Also, becoming FWB after being in a relationship is going backwards and doesn't work!

Q: I want to propose to my girlfriend but I'm hesitant. The problem is, she cheated on her ex with me…so I know she's capable of cheating and that's always on the back of my mind. Should I trust her?

A: You'd have to make a decision to just trust her. If you don't, you won't have a healthy relationship. You probably should've thought about this before getting to the point of proposal. If you can't do it, then you shouldn't propose to her and just try to move on.

Q: My current girlfriend started a new job where my ex works. I'm terrified that my ex and she will get too close and my girlfriend will leave me. What should I do?

A: I understand why this makes you uncomfortable, but I don't think this will cause your girlfriend to leave you.
Have a talk with her and ask her to make sure she maintains a healthy distance from your ex. I doubt she plans on being her bestie anyway.

Chapter 5 Playlist

BOO THANG - VERSE SIMMONDS

RESPECT - ARETHA FRANKLIN

PYT - MICHAEL JACKSON

HEART ATTACK - DEMI LOVATO

IN COMMON - ALICIA KEYS

UNTHINKABLE - ALICIA KEYS

Serious Relationships

"If passionate love is the coke of love, companionate love is like having a glass of wine or smoking a few hits of some mild weed."

— Aziz Ansari

S erious relationships can be great if you're in the right one. They cultivate feelings of love, security, consistency, and comfort. It is always so nice to see couples who are in serious relationships prosper and truly enjoy each other's company. It's so cute (and sometimes nauseating) to see two people in love packing on the PDA! They should keep the kissing noises down though...because ew! 🤢

Anyway, when you're in a relationship, your significant other should also be your friend! You spend most of your time and emotional energy on this person, so it's important to make sure you actually *like* them! I know that seems like an obvious statement, but believe me when I tell you, *it is possible to love someone and not like them*. I've been there.

While these kind of relationships can be all rainbows, butterflies, and everything wonderful, they can also be the opposite. They come with complications, compromise, and bumps in the road. However, there are so many exciting and scary milestones in relationships, like saying "I love you" for the first time, meeting the parents, moving in together, etc. that make all the bad stuff worth it.

There are some special cases, though, that are totally unhealthy for all parties involved. It is best to exit these relationships. If you're in a situation where there is any kind of abuse, you need to leave as soon as possible. There are people and places to go to for help. Let the people who love you know what's going on. Friends, family, and professionals can help you through.

10 Best Things about
Being in a Serious Relationship

 You can say you're unavailable and mean it when someone you're not interested in at all approaches you in public.

 You develop your own relationship language with inside jokes and things only you two understand. I've had secret handshakes, made up words and sounds, and facial expressions that all meant something in our own weird language in my past relationships.

 You have an awesome excuse to get out of anything. "I have to go, my girlfriend is locked out of her apartment. Gotta help her out." Or, "I can't make it to your birthday dinner! My boyfriend isn't feeling well so I'm playing nurse tonight."

 You always have someone to have sex with. Your boyfriend or girlfriend is usually a sure thing.

 You feel safe and secure knowing that you have a shoulder to lean on no matter what happens that day.

If you don't get a text back right away, it's no big deal. You'll see your boo at home or at the date night you guys already planned yesterday.

 You get to perfect and combine your kissing styles so that there's never a gross or bad make out session.

 You always have someone on your side and rooting for you, so when they tell you something you did or are doing looks dumb, you trust them because you know they want the best for you.

 You have someone to take care of you when you're under the weather. No more trucking it to the pharmacy for flu medicine and soup when you're half dead in the freezing cold. I love when my S.O. plays doctor!

 You have someone to stand up for you when you're backed into a corner by friends or family members. You're a unit and no one messes with one without messing with the other!

Q: Is there a sign that means you're in a serious relationship? Like I think the guy I'm seeing and I are serious, but I keep thinking back to that scene in *500 Days of Summer* where they have a big fight when they try to define their relationship... you know what I mean? It's a scary conversation and I don't want to rock the boat.

A: It is ideal to be on the same page with your S.O. There's nothing wrong with wanting to know the general direction of where things are headed. Neither of you should continue to invest valuable time if you don't agree on the stipulations of your relationship.

Q: Why is it that all the good guys are in serious relationships?

A: Because they're good guys.

Q: When do you know if you are ready to propose?

A: I'm not sure. I haven't done any proposing. I've only been proposed to. But if you can't imagine fighting with anyone else about constantly leaving the cap off the toothpaste, then they could possibly be the one.

Q: What's the key to making a relationship last? I can't seem to get passed a few dates.

A: If you can't make it past a few dates, there's probably not much chemistry between you and your dates. However, when you're in an actual relationship, compromise and understanding are huge factors in the longevity of the relationship. You have to let them pick the movie sometimes and share holidays between your families.

Q: How can I tell if my boyfriend is getting ready to propose? I want him to do it already, but I don't want to come off as pushy? Are there any hints I can give off for him to propose… or will that come off as pushy?

A: You shouldn't constantly drop hints. He should know you eventually want that, but you don't need to force it. It'll happen at the right time when you are both ready.

Q: So I'm ready to propose and I don't know where to begin. Do you have any tips for picking a ring? How important is the actual proposal?

A: You'll need some help from her mom, sister, or best friend. They'll be able to help you pick something she'd like because I am sure she's mentioned her ring preferences to them a few *thousand* times. For ring size, steal a ring she always wears and bring it to the jeweler.

The proposal is important, but what really matters is how thoughtful it is as opposed to extravagant.

Q: I've met his parents and vice-versa. It was kinda awkward and uncomfortable. Now our parents are going to meet each other. Anything you can suggest to make it a little more relaxed?

A: Yes! Make sure this meeting involves music, food, and drinks. That way, there's a lot of eating and less talking. 😊 Before you know it, it's been 3 hours, they've said 25 words to each other, and it's time for everyone to go home with full bellies and smiles on their faces.

"Before you marry someone you should first make them use a computer with slow internet to see who they really are."

— Will Ferrell

Q: I think I want to ask my girlfriend to move in with me. But what if she says no? Is it too soon? We've been together 6 months.

A: I do not recommend moving in after only being together for 6 months. You barely know each other! You'll never regret taking it slow.

Q: How do we balance finances in a relationship? My boyfriend has shitty credit but he's a great guy... is that enough to end it?

A: Why would you end it over something that can be worked on and improved? A bad credit score isn't the end of the world. However, if he has a gambling problem or other financial vices, you may want to reconsider staying in the relationship.

Q: My girlfriend still has "single" on her Facebook page. We've been together for 8 months. She says it's so her parents won't bug her about it. We're away at college and she's not allowed to date. But it drives me crazy that she's scared of her parents... and my parents and friends rag on me that she doesn't take me seriously. How do I get her to commit to being Facebook official?

A: If she really likes you, she won't continue to keep you a secret from all of Facebook. If you have a talk with her about this and she still won't budge, it could be time to break up. For all you know, she could have multiple boyfriends. 😕 Someone who's really into you and has nothing to hide won't keep you hidden for long.

Q: A little silly, but when we first started dating, my boyfriend would always post pics of us on Instagram. He now never posts pics of us. Is he tired of me?

A: As I said in the previous answer, when you're with someone you truly love or like, you want to profess your affection and feelings about them. Instagram isn't the be-all, end-all of relationships, though. Does he treat you well in real life? Is he kind, thoughtful, and attentive? Some people just aren't always active online.

Chapter 6 Playlist

EMOTIONS - MARIAH CAREY

I'M SPRUNG - T PAIN

WHAT YOU WON'T DO FOR LOVE - BOBBY CALDWELL

EVERYONE FALLS IN LOVE - TANTO METRO

WHEN A MAN LOVES A WOMAN - MICHAEL BOLTON

TWO OCCASIONS - BABYFACE

PRIME TIME - JANELLE MONAE FT. MIGUEL

MY GIRL - THE TEMPTATIONS

JUST THE TWO OF US - GROVER WASHINGTON

BY YOUR SIDE - SADE

ALL MY LIFE - KC & JOJO

Chapter 7

Dating Lisa

"There are only three things women need in life: food, water, and compliments."

— *Chris Rock*

I am so glad you read this far. Really, thank you. That means at least one person read my book and that is more than I could have imagined. Anyway, I really hope I was helpful in some way and that you enjoyed what I had to say. Truly, that is the primary reason I wrote this book. I am happy you got to know me a bit and hope we can keep being friends. Like, are you going to text me tomorrow? I mean, you don't have to... but we've spent so much time together that I hope that you'd want to keep in touch! No pressure, though. Really... Just call me whenever! Or like, every day. So um, yeah. I'll miss you... 🫣

Haha! I am joking but I *really am* glad you read this book. I promise the previous paragraph is not a glimpse of what it's like to date me. At least, I don't think so. One thing people have said about dating me is that I can sometimes talk so much and so fast all at once that it's hard to keep up with me. I'm naturally inquisitive, so I'm known to ask a million questions in one millisecond and expect answers immediately. I think it's a Dominican thing or a Latin thing but I'm not exactly sure.

If that's how fast I talk, imagine how fast I think! I can jump to a conclusion faster than a speeding bullet. One good thing about dating me is that I always have snacks because I'm *always* hungry. So anyone who dates me is never hungry but always sleepy. That's good, right?

Lisa's Loves:

The Good, the Bad, &
the Wacky

* I once dated a guy who sent me unsolicited photos of his feet. It was really weird. He was like, "Hey! Hope you're having a good weekend!" *sends photo of feet* I just ignored him. There was no way he was getting pictures of my feet in return. I think that's what he was hoping.

* My favorite thing about dating is the cute and thoughtful gestures that come with getting to know each other. I never forget meaningful gifts or occurrences. The only people from the past I miss are the ones who remembered the little things about me.

* I dated someone who had such a severe lying problem, he would even lie about the smallest things, like what he had for dinner or what he did earlier that day. It was very bizarre and frustrating.

* While on a first date with someone, we got into a lighthearted debate about something trivial. He wanted to prove me wrong with a google search. When he opened his browser and began to type in the search bar, the recent searches included "Lisa Ramos sexy", "Lisa Ramos boyfriend", "Lisa Ramos hot" and a few more along those lines. I pretended not to notice, but I definitely saw them all!

* I caught someone looking through my phone after only two dates. I was furious. He has no idea I know, but I have a little trick that tells me when someone has been on my phone when I've left it unattended.

Worst Pick-up Lines
I've Actually Heard
(aka What Not to Do)

* "Did you know that 'embargo' spelled backwards is 'o grab me'?"

* "You look like my future ex-wife."

* "Do you like pancakes? How about iHop on that ass?

* "You seem like the kinda girl that's heard every line in the book... How about just one more?"

* "Is your name Wi-Fi? Because we definitely have a connection."

* "Thank God I brought my library card because I am totally checking you out."

* "Are you a beaver? Because Dam!"

* "You turn my software into hardware."

* "I want to cover you in peanut butter and lick you until my peanut allergy kills me."

* "Is your ass from McDonald's? Because I'm lovin' it."

* "Are you my appendix? Because I don't know how you work, but this feeling in my stomach makes me want to take you out."

* "Your profile pic won't load, but your pixelated pic makes you look like a really sexy Lego."

* "I may not be the hottest guy here, but I'm the only one talking to you."

Q: What does a girl like you look for in a guy?

A: I like when a man is well-spoken and intelligent. Good conversation is very important to me. I also like lighthearted, playful personalities. All the guys I've really liked have made me laugh 'til I cried.

Q: Do you have a type?

A: Not really, honestly! None of the guys I've dated have much in common.

Q: Have you ever tried online dating?

A: I personally haven't done the online dating thing but I have friends who use all these dating apps and they seem to love it. In my opinion, it's more fun to meet people organically. I've met people through friends, while I'm out, at the gym, etc. It's nice to have a face-to-face introduction before an actual date.

Q: If I come to NY, will you go on a date with me?

A: No. I don't like blind dates. I need to be able to stalk someone's Instagram and Twitter beforehand. ☺

Q: What do you think about Zac Efron? Would you date him?

A: I don't really have an opinion about Zac Efron. We could go on one date though, maybe get some pizza at Chuck E. Cheese.

Q: If I dared you to kiss me, would you?

A: # Nope.

Q: What does a guy have to do to get you to go on a date with him?

A: Ask! I've had so many people say they've wanted to talk to me long before they actually did. If you want to go out on a date with someone, you never will if you don't ask. The answer may be "no", but who cares? If it's a "yes", you'll be glad you did.

Q: How would someone get to know the real you? I would imagine with your celebrity status you don't get too many people coming up to you just to get to know you or am I wrong?

A: The only way someone can really get to know me is by spending time with and talking to me. That's the only way people get to know each other. I think the only people who have gotten to really know me (besides my friends and family) are the people I've been on more than 3 dates with. Anyone who hasn't spent more than that amount of time with me doesn't know me well at all.

Q: What's your dream meal to have on a first date?

A: Comfort food! 😋 I love comfort food. My mood is always enhanced when I'm eating something horribly delicious.

Q: What is your idea of a dream date?

A: I want to meet a baby monkey or a micro mini pig. I haven't done that yet. I also love blue roses, so some of those should be involved. There should be definitely be food. I also love scary movies. I don't know. I'm just throwing stuff out there. I don't have a specific dream date in mind. Just be nice to me and make sure I'm fed every few hours. I'm never happy unless there's food involved.

Q: Have you ever been heartbroken?

A: I've *definitely* been heartbroken. It was awful. The term "heartbreak" comes from the occurrence of feeling actual pain in your chest when you're experiencing extreme emotional pain. I did not believe it was possible until it happened to me. I did some research and learned that emotional and physical pain involve the same region of the brain. Isn't that nuts? I did lose about 10 pounds, so that was an upside! I'm joking, of course.

Q: What is the longest relationship you've ever been in?

A: I've been in two 4-year-long relationships.

Q: Would it matter if a guy is younger than you?

A: Maturity and life experience are more important to me. I know 30 year olds who act like they're 18 and I know 23 year olds who act like they're 40. In *some* cases, age really is just a number. However, I do think it's a good idea to date close to your age or a bit older. I've never dated anyone more than 10 years older.

✧ Lisa's Favorite Jams ✧

MY FAVORITE TV SHOW THEME SONG
FROM CHILDHOOD:

WITH A LITTLE HELP FROM MY FRIENDS -
JOE COCKER *(The Wonder Years)*

MY FAVORITE SONG AS A TEENAGE FANGIRL:

I WANT IT THAT WAY - BACK STREET BOYS
(My favorite one was Brian!)

A SONG THAT REMINDS ME OF MY FIRST CRUSH:
ONE CALL AWAY - CHINGY

A SONG THAT REMINDS ME OF MY
FIRST BOYFRIEND:
WONDERWALL - OASIS

A SONG THAT REMINDS ME OF JR HIGH:
TIPSY - J KWON

FIRST SONG PLAYED AT MY PROM:
BUY YOU A DRANK - T PAIN

SONG THAT PUTS ME IN A GOOD MOOD
EVERY TIME:
LET'S DO IT AGAIN - J BOOG

SONG THAT HELPED ME GET THROUGH MY
FIRST REAL HEARTBREAK:
SAY SOMETHING - TIMBALAND

FAVORITE BEATLES SONG:
IN MY LIFE - THE BEATLES

FAVORITE BIGGIE SONG:
THE WARNING - BIGGIE

FAVORITE GOSPEL SONG:
DESERT SONG

FAVORITE DISNEY SONG:
BEAUTY AND THE BEAST

To me, every guy is like a pizza pie!

Sort of...

Think about it. The classic. A quick delivery, late night **Cheese pizza** is not blowing the doors off any restaurant, but it has its place in the foodie world. Get your mind out of the gutter. This classic isn't a booty call. No, a classic cheese pizza is the guy with zero game, a bland personality but a heart of gold.
They're the friend who is good for listening to you talk about the guy you like or the ex you're hung up on. Cheese pizza is comfort.

Then there is **Mr. Extra Cheese** (in every sense of the word). They're cheesy, corny, and too much to handle if you're lactose-intolerant. Cheese, like all things in life, is great in moderation. Except for wine. Wine is just great.

 As you move through the menu of pizzas, you come across the meats. Oh the **Meat-Lovers**, how I loathe you. It's a love/hate relationship with these guys. They're easy on the eyes but difficult at times to work with. These meatheads want to dominate all the other toppings, when the truth is, the crust is just as important.

#pizzaovergainz

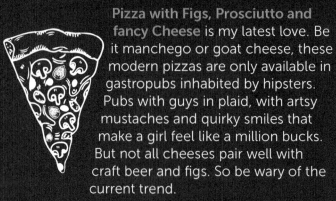

Pizza with Figs, Prosciutto and fancy Cheese is my latest love. Be it manchego or goat cheese, these modern pizzas are only available in gastropubs inhabited by hipsters. Pubs with guys in plaid, with artsy mustaches and quirky smiles that make a girl feel like a million bucks. But not all cheeses pair well with craft beer and figs. So be wary of the current trend.

Hawaiian pizza, the AC Slater of the food world. He's the dream, the fantasy, the one we all think about at some point but only share with our friends. The one that is too exotic for some but perfect for others.

Pepperoni, the security blanket. The go-to that makes everyone at a party happy. They're the guy next door. The guy that can be paired with a coke or a beer or a cocktail. They're respectful yet flirty, and can definitely get a little spicy if the mood is right.

Dating Quiz

Now that you have all my insights, tips and tricks for how to (and how not to) date, I think it's time we look in the mirror. A topic I wrote about earlier was on 'dating yourself.' While it may seem cliché and something your mom would tell you after a bad breakup, the truth is it's needed. We all need to learn to love ourselves before we can share that love with anyone else. And the only way to love ourselves is to understand who we are. So I devised this quiz to test all the ins and outs of our inner most thoughts in order to find out what you're looking for in an ideal date.

Have fun, fill it out, and be HONEST. It might help to have a glass of wine or a slice of pizza as you get started. At the end of the quiz use the key to help you determine how you tested and what kind of date makes the most sense for you.

Section 1: Getting to Know Yourself

1. Are you a morning person?

___ **A.** Yes. I get out of bed and am ready to face the day.

✓ **B.** I can manage it, but rather not.

___ **C.** I'm not getting up before 11 am.

___ **D.** #nightowl.

2. How would you describe your everyday look?

___ **A.** I try, but not too hard.

___ **B.** Boring but comfortable.

___ **C.** People notice when I walk into a room.

✓ **D.** Black. I love wearing black.

3. Which part of you would you say people notice most ?

✓ **A.** Personality.

___ **B.** Physical body.

___ **C.** My clothes and style.

___ **D.** Neither, I'm like a shadow.

4. Animated films, what team are you?

√ **A.** Disney.

___ **B.** Studio Ghibli.

___ **C.** Pixar.

___ **D.** DreamWorks.

5. Your ideal plans on a Friday night are?

√ **A.** A double-date or social gathering with my partner.

___ **B.** Happy hour with friends and co-workers.

___ **C.** A dinner date at a romantic spot.

___ **D.** At home, on the couch with your pup and the first 9 seasons of your favorite show.

6. You're headed to a house party. Who will you be spotted with?

√ **A.** The people you came with.

___ **B.** Mingling with strangers.

___ **C.** The most attractive person in the room.

___ **D.** Me, myself and I.

7. The TV power-couple you envy the most is?

___ **A.** Mitchell and Cameron, "Modern Family".

___ **B.** Marshall and Lily, "How I Met Your Mother".

✓ **C.** Cory and Topanga, "Boy Meets World".

___ **D.** Tina Belcher and Jimmy Pesto Jr., "Bob's Burgers".

8. Favorite meal of the day?

___ **A.** Dinner.

✓ **B.** Brunch.

___ **C.** Lunch.

___ **D.** Taco Bell's Fourth Meal ™.

9. What makes a great date?

___ **A.** A passionate kiss.

___ **B.** An outdoor activity.

✓ **C.** The best meal ever.

___ **D.** Alcohol.

10. Vegetarian, Meat Lover, or Food Lover?

___ **A.** A mix of everything.

___ **B.** Only eat meat or only vegetables.

_✓_ **C.** Incredibly picky eater.

___ **D.** Cereal, Hot Pockets and Klondike Bars.

Section 2: How Would You Act?

1. You, your mom and your dad are walking through a park and you see teenagers making out on a bench. How does that make you feel?

___ **A.** It makes me happy to see young love.

___ **B.** It makes me uneasy to see it.

_✓_ **C.** So long as it's PG, I'm cool with it.

___ **D.** Parks scare me. I rather stay home.

2. You're on a date and it's been quiet for the last 10 minutes. How does that make you feel?

___ **A.** As long as they're not ignoring me to be on their phone, I don't mind.

✓ **B.** Weird and uncomfortable.

___ **C.** It could be worse, they could be rambling on for hours I guess.

___ **D.** Awkward silences make me very happy.

3. Your best friend and your partner hit it off. Are you okay with it?

___ **A.** Thrilled.

___ **B.** No, I'm a bit resentful.

___ **C.** Don't really care.

✓ **D.** My best friend is my dog. Everybody loves my dog.

4. Your partner suggests that you guys take a weekend apart every so often. Are you okay with this?

✓ **A.** It's nice to take time away occasionally.

___ **B.** Absolutely love it. Makes us feel closer.

___ **C.** So long as we've talked about it and are clear on the details.

___ **D.** No, no, no.

5. The last few weeks have been hectic and the relationship seems very unsteady. What's your plan of action?

___ **A.** I would suggest a therapist.

___ **B.** Ignore it. Like all things in life, there are highs and lows.

✓ **C.** Try my hardest to fix it.

___ **D.** Just run and never look back, #failfast.

6. Your partner is nervous to introduce you to their parents. How does this make you feel?

___ **A.** Upset.

___ **B.** Confused.

✓ **C.** Understanding.

___ **D.** It's irrelevant to me, they have their reasons for being nervous.

7. Your partner's parents do not approve of you. What do you think of that?

___ **A.** It's the 21st century, we don't need their approval.

✓ **B.** I wish we had it. But with time, they'll see I'm the right person for their son/daughter.

___ **C.** It's keeping me up at night.

___ **D.** Well, I don't like them.

8. Your partner suggests a kinky idea for the bedroom...your thoughts?

✓ **A.** I'm 100% on board.

___ **B.** Depends how 'kinky' the suggestion is. Some things are off-limits.

___ **C.** Not interested.

___ **D.** Every night should be kinky.

9. Your partner admits to being unfaithful. What's your initial reaction?

✓ **A.** I'm hurt and it will take time, but we might make it.

___ **B.** It's over, I could never trust them again.

___ **C.** It happens. We're not married, we just need to communicate better.

___ **D.** The fact that they would cheat on me speaks volumes.

10. There's an outfit you're dying for, but you know your partner won't like it...do you get it?

___ **A.** Yes.

___ **B.** No.

✓ **C.** Depends on why I'm buying the outfit.

___ **D.** After they see me in it, they'll change their mind.

Self-Assessment

Now that the quiz is behind us, let's see how you did. Tally up all your answers and then compare them to the chart below:

If most of your answers were **A, you are ready for a committed relationship.**

If most of your answers were **B, keep enjoying the single life.**

If most of your answers were **C, caught in the middle of wanting a serious relationship, but loving your freedom.**

If most of your answers were **D, WTF? you might want to retake the quiz**

The last thing I want to leave you with is your very own **Pizza and Chill** journal. After digesting this book, I think you're ready to hit the dating scene. Like all of us, you're going to have some hits and some misses. But the most important thing is to keep laughing and keep learning.

Use the following pages to keep track of your favorite dates, the disaster dates and the ones that surprised you (good or bad). As you may have noticed from the theme of my book, we live in a very digital world. However, sometimes it's good to take a step back and appreciate some of the more old-fashioned aspects of life. Like when a guy would formally ask girls out on a date.

Here's to less 'pizza and chill' texts and more memorable dates!

Pizza & Chill Journal

Favorite dates

Disaster dates

Dates that surprised you (good or bad)

Closing

Thank you so much for reading! I hope you enjoyed hanging out with me.

Hopefully we've found some common ground and can agree that modern dating is weird, exciting, annoying, fun and confusing sometimes! We are all on a very similar roller coaster ride. The good news is that there is someone out there for everyone and every experience you have now brings you closer to meeting someone awesome. There's always something to learn when dating, and you'll never regret being kind, respectful, and taking the high road.

Best of luck to you all! Let's keep in touch! Tweet me or somethin'! 😶

xoxo, Lisa

Lisa Ramos

Author Bio

Lisa Ramos is a Dominican-American model best known as an expert panelist on MTV's popular comedic series *Guy Code*. The show features Ramos as she voices her opinion and offers advice to men and women about various topics on dating. After three successful seasons as a panelist, she moved on to co-produce her own comedic web series with Univision's first bilingual network, The Flama, called the *Secret Life of Babes*. The series features Ramos as the primary host and actress as she hilariously narrates the episodes about the strange world of dating. Her uncanny ability to relate and connect to people through her hilarious personal experiences has led her to a rapidly increasing and loyal following. Ramos currently lives in New York City and continues to build her brand through hard work, charisma and dedication.

CPSIA information can be obtained at www.ICGtesting.com
Printed in the USA
BVOW05s1955150916

462243BV00006B/6/P

9 781633 533868